# Practical
# Tex-Mex

$p^3$

This is a P³ Book
First published in 2003

P³
Queen Street House
4 Queen Street
Bath BA1 1HE, UK

ISBN: 1-40540-931-2

Printed in China

**NOTE**

This book uses metric and imperial measurements. Follow the same units
of measurement throughout; do not mix metric and imperial.
All spoon measurements are level: teaspoons are assumed to be 5 ml, and
tablespoons are assumed to be 15 ml. Unless otherwise stated,
milk is assumed to be full fat, eggs and individual vegetables such as potatoes
are medium, and pepper is freshly ground black pepper.

The nutritional information provided for each recipe is per serving or per person.
Optional ingredients, variations, or serving suggestions have
not been included in the calculations. The times given for each recipe are an approximate
guide only because the preparation times may differ according to the techniques used by
different people and the cooking times may vary as a result of the type of oven used.

Recipes using raw or very lightly cooked eggs should be
avoided by children, the elderly, pregnant women, convalescents,
and anyone suffering from an illness.

# Contents

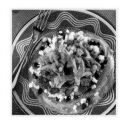

# Introduction

Tex-Mex, the name given to the cookery of northern Mexico and the south-western USA, is a fusion food with ancient origins. To unravel its different elements, consider first that Texas, now on the border with Mexico, was actually part of Mexico until 1836. This area had been explored and conquered by the Spanish between the 16th and 17th centuries, and before that, the Aztecs dominated much of Mexico. But the cultural mix does not end there. You need to throw in contributions from the Native Americans and cowboys for good measure. Today, Tex-Mex cookery is still evolving and is becoming ever more popular.

### Tex-Mex classics

There are a few dishes that are fundamentally Tex-Mex, which have been developed, adapted, and adopted by successive generations:

**Chilli con carne** This translates as 'chilli with meat', although to many Texans it is known as 'bowl of red'. Arguments rage as to exactly what constitutes an 'authentic' rendering of the dish. Should the beef be minced or cut into cubes? Traditionalists insist on the latter. Do you add beans? Are they mixed in or served on the side? Then we come to the heart of the debate – should it be made with chilli powder (a seasoning that combines dried chillies, cumin seeds, oregano and garlic) or just whole chillies? Some variations call for tomatoes (either ripe or green) and red peppers, while purists denounce the use of any vegetables, including onion. But in the end, it is entirely down to personal preference. One delicious twist on the 'original' concoction is to add a couple of squares or so of continental plain chocolate, which lends a hint of sweetness and a dark richness to the sauce – after all, the Aztecs did introduce cocoa to Mexico.

**Guacamole** This dish is served as a dip, topping or sauce, and has as many different variations as there are cooks. The avocado is the only ingredient not in dispute, with one or all of the following in contention – garlic, finely chopped shallot or spring onion, chopped tomato, and coriander. There is then a divide between those who use lemon juice and those who prefer lime. The nature and strength of the seasoning also varies, from finely chopped fresh green chilli to chilli powder, red pepper and Tabasco sauce. Texture is another issue: some prefer their guacamole relatively coarse, and mix the ingredients by hand instead of mixing them in a food processor to a smooth consistency. Look no further than the recipe on page 13 for a traditional version of this versatile dish. Remember that the avocado in guacamole will quickly discolour, although the lemon or lime juice will slow down the process, so cover it tightly with clingfilm.

**Salsa** This means 'sauce' in Spanish, and is the staple condiment of Tex-Mex cookery. Traditionally a salsa is tomato-based and highly seasoned, although many different varieties of salsa now abound in Tex-Mex cookery and use a whole range of ingredients. 'Salsa cruda' indicates an uncooked mixture, in which raw ingredients are finely chopped, instead of puréed, to give a chunky texture, but salsas can also be cooked. A classic type is salsa verde, which is based on a combination of green ingredients, usually tomatillos, green chillies and coriander. Pico de gallo, which means 'rooster's beak' in Spanish, is a famous uncooked salsa that customarily includes jícama (Mexican potato), cucumbers, peppers, onions, oranges and jalapeño chillies. Salsas can be used in dishes to add extra flavour, and are delicious served as a dip with tortilla chips. Being low in fat and calories, they are also a healthy option.

## Tex-Mex glossary

For those people who do not yet know their enchilada from their empanada, or their tortilla from their tostada, here are explanations of the terms and ingredients most likely to be found in Tex-Mex cookery:

**Albóndigas** Meatballs.

**Barbacoa** Grilled meat (origin of the word 'barbecue').

**Burrito** Meaning 'little donkey', a large flour tortilla enclosing a filling, usually bean-based but can be meat.

**Chillies rellenos** Mild, green chillies stuffed with cheese, dipped in batter, and fried until crisp and the cheese melts.

**Chimichanga** A fried or deep-fried burrito.

**Chorizo** A sausage of coarsely minced fresh or smoked pork, flavoured with garlic, chilli powder and other spices.

**Churro** A spiral of sweet dough, coated in cinnamon and sugar and deep-fried.

**Empanada** Pastry turnover with a meat, vegetable or fruit filling.

**Enchilada** A soft corn tortilla rolled round a cheese, meat or other savoury filling, topped with salsa and cheese.

**Fajitas** Traditionally strips of beef skirt steak, marinated in oil and spices, barbecued and cut into strips. Usually served wrapped in warm tortillas.

**Mole** A rich, dark sauce traditionally served with chicken, usually containing chicken stock, ground seeds or nuts, chillies and continental plain chocolate.

**Quesadilla** A flour tortilla with a savoury filling, often cheese, folded in half to form a turnover shape and then grilled or fried.

**Taco** A corn tortilla – generally the crisp variety in Tex-Mex cookery – encasing a savoury filling.

**Tomatillo** The tomatillo is small, green and tomato-like but with a papery casing like a cape gooseberry, and has a fragrant lemony apple flavour.

**Tortilla** A round, flat, thin bread made with either wheat flour or corn flour.

**Tostada** A fried corn tortilla topped with ingredients such as refried beans, shredded beef or chicken, lettuce, tomatoes, cheese, soured cream, or guacamole.

## Chilli know-how

There are over 200 varieties of chilli, more than half of which originate from Mexico. They vary in colour, from yellow to black, and heat intensity, from mild to scorching. Generally, the smaller the chilli, the hotter it is likely to be. The following types of chilli are the most popular:

**Ancho** This is the most widely used dried chilli, broad, reddish-brown, with a sweet, slightly fruity flavour. It is called a poblano chilli in its fresh, green state, which is the favourite choice for chillies rellenos (stuffed chillies).

**Chipotle** A dried, smoked jalapeño chilli, brown and hot.

**Habañero** This lantern-shaped green, yellow or orange chilli is as hot as they come.

**Jalapeño** This 5-cm/2-inch long, hot to very hot chilli is often used in its fresh, green state before it ripens to red.

**Mulato** A long, dark brown, dried type of poblano chilli with a smoky flavour, traditionally used for making mole.

**Pasilla** Also called chilli negro, this is a long, thin, brown-black, medium-hot dried chilli, also available powdered.

**Serrano** A small, green, very hot chilli, maturing to a sweeter red, then yellow.

Take great care when preparing hot chillies to prevent them burning your skin and eyes. Use protective gloves – the thin plastic kind available from chemists are more practical than less flexible rubber gloves. The white membranes are the hottest part of a chilli, but the seeds are also fiery, so remove both if you want a milder flavour. Beware when cooking hot fresh chillies over a high heat – their fumes can irritate your lungs, throat, nose and eyes.

To cool a dish that is too hot, or to soothe a burning mouth, add or eat plain yogurt or soured cream.

## KEY

 Simplicity level 1–3 (1 easiest, 3 slightly harder)

 Preparation time

 Cooking time

# Mexican Vegetable Soup

Crisp tortilla chips act as croûtons in this hearty vegetable soup, which is found throughout Mexico. Add cheese to melt in, if you wish.

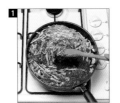

## NUTRITIONAL INFORMATION

| | | | |
|---|---|---|---|
| Calories | .......201 | Sugars | .........9g |
| Protein | .........6g | Fat | ...........9g |
| Carbohydrate | ...27g | Saturates | .......1g |

 10 mins     40 mins

### SERVES 4

## I N G R E D I E N T S

2 tbsp vegetable oil or extra-virgin olive oil

1 onion, finely chopped

4 garlic cloves, finely chopped

¼–½ tsp ground cumin

2–3 tsp mild chilli powder

1 carrot, sliced

1 waxy potato, diced

350 g/12 oz diced fresh or
   canned tomatoes

1 courgette, diced

¼ small cabbage, shredded

1 litre/1¾ pints vegetable or chicken
   stock or water

1 corn cob, the kernels cut off the cob or
   225 g/8 oz drained canned sweetcorn

about 10 French beans, cut into bite-
   sized lengths

salt and pepper

### TO SERVE

4–6 tbsp chopped fresh coriander

salsa of your choice or chopped fresh chilli,
   to taste

tortilla chips

1 Heat the oil in a heavy-based frying pan. Add the onion and garlic and cook for a few minutes until softened, then sprinkle in the cumin and chilli powder. Stir in the carrot, potato, tomatoes, courgette and cabbage and cook, stirring occasionally, for 2 minutes.

2 Pour in the stock. Cover and cook over a medium heat for 20 minutes until the vegetables are tender.

3 Add extra water if necessary, then stir in the sweetcorn and French beans and cook for another 5–10 minutes, or until the beans are tender. Season with salt and pepper to taste, bearing in mind that the tortilla chips may be salty.

4 Ladle the soup into soup bowls and sprinkle each portion with chopped fresh coriander. Top with a spoonful of salsa, then add a handful of tortilla chips.

# Tortas

Throughout Mexico you will find street vendors selling these substantial Mexican rolls. Make your own and vary the filling as you wish.

## NUTRITIONAL INFORMATION

| | |
|---|---|
| Calories . . . . . . .544 | Sugars . . . . . . . . .6g |
| Protein . . . . . . . .29g | Fat . . . . . . . . . .31g |
| Carbohydrate . . .38g | Saturates . . . . .13g |

 10 mins     4–5 mins

### SERVES 4

## I N G R E D I E N T S

4 crusty rolls, such as French rolls
  or bocadillos

melted butter or olive oil, for brushing

225 g/8 oz canned refried beans

350 g/12 oz shredded cooked chicken,
  browned chorizo pieces, sliced ham and
  cheese, or any leftover cooked meat you
  have to hand

1 ripe tomato, sliced or diced

1 small onion, finely chopped

2 tbsp chopped fresh coriander

1 avocado, stoned, sliced, and tossed with
  lime juice

4–6 tbsp soured cream or Greek yogurt

salsa of your choice

handful of shredded lettuce

1 Cut the rolls in half. Remove a little of the crumb to make space for the filling.

2 Brush the outside and inside of the rolls with butter or olive oil, and toast, on both sides, on a hot griddle or frying pan for a few minutes until crisp. Alternatively, place in a preheated oven at 200°C/400°F/Gas Mark 6 until lightly toasted.

3 Meanwhile, place the beans in a saucepan with a tiny amount of water and heat through gently.

4 When the rolls are heated, spread one half of each roll generously with the beans, then top with a layer of cooked meat. Top with tomato, onion, fresh coriander and avocado.

5 Generously spread soured cream or yogurt on to the other side of each roll. Spoon the salsa over the filling, add a little shredded lettuce, then sandwich the two sides of each roll together and press tightly. Serve immediately.

### VARIATION
Add any Mexican sauce, such as Mild Red Chilli Sauce (see page 15), to the meat filling to vary the flavour.

# Cheese & Bean Quesadillas

These bite-sized rolls are made from flour tortillas filled with a delicious mixture of refried beans, melted cheese, coriander and salsa.

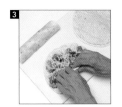

| NUTRITIONAL INFORMATION | |
|---|---|
| Calories .......452 | Sugars ........11g |
| Protein ........18g | Fat ..........16g |
| Carbohydrate ...62g | Saturates .......7g |

 10 mins     10 mins

### SERVES 4–6

## I N G R E D I E N T S

400 g/14 oz canned refried beans

8 flour tortillas

oil, for greasing

200 g/7 oz Cheddar cheese, grated

1 onion, chopped

½ bunch of fresh coriander leaves, chopped

1 quantity Salsa Cruda (see page 16)

sprigs of fresh parsley, to garnish

1 Place the beans in a small pan and set over a low heat to warm through.

2 Meanwhile, warm the tortillas gently in a lightly greased, non-stick frying pan.

3 Remove the tortillas from the pan and quickly spread with a layer of warm beans. Top each tortilla with grated cheese, chopped onion, fresh coriander and a spoonful of salsa. Roll up tightly.

4 Just before serving, heat the non-stick frying pan over a medium heat,

sprinkling lightly with a couple of drops of water. Add the tortilla rolls, cover the pan, and heat through until the cheese melts. Let them brown lightly, if you wish.

5 Remove the tortilla rolls from the pan and slice each roll diagonally into about 4 bite-sized pieces. Serve the quesadillas at once.

## COOK'S TIP

Flour tortillas can also be warmed in the microwave, but take care not to heat them for too long because they can become leathery.

# Black Bean Nachos

This tasty black bean and cheese dip is packed with authentic Mexican flavours and will get any meal off to a good start.

## NUTRITIONAL INFORMATION

| | | | |
|---|---|---|---|
| Calories | .......429 | Sugars | .........2g |
| Protein | ........28g | Fat | ..........24g |
| Carbohydrate | ...25g | Saturates | ......15g |

10 mins, plus 8 hrs soaking    1¾ hrs

### SERVES 4

## INGREDIENTS

225 g/8 oz dried black beans, or canned black beans, drained and rinsed

175–225 g/6–8 oz grated cheese, such as Cheddar, Asiago, fontina, pecorino or a combination

about ¼ tsp cumin seeds or ground cumin

about 4 tbsp soured cream

pickled jalapeño chillies, thinly sliced (optional)

1 tbsp chopped fresh coriander

handful of shredded lettuce

tortilla chips, to serve

1 If using dried black beans, place them in a bowl and add water to cover. Set aside to soak overnight, then drain. Put in a saucepan, cover with water and bring to the boil. Boil for 10 minutes, then lower the heat and simmer for about 1½ hours until tender. Drain well.

2 Spread the cooked or canned beans in the bottom of a shallow casserole, then sprinkle the cheese over the top. Sprinkle with cumin to taste.

3 Bake in a preheated oven, 190°C/ 375°F/Gas Mark 5, for 10–15 minutes or until the beans are cooked through and the cheese is bubbling and melted.

4 Remove the beans and cheese from the oven and spoon the soured cream on top. Add the jalapeño chillies, if using, and sprinkle with coriander and lettuce.

5 Arrange the tortilla chips around the beans, sticking them into the mixture. Serve the nachos at once.

### VARIATION
To add a meaty flavour, spoon chopped and browned chorizo on top of the beans before sprinkling over the cheese, and cook as in step 3 – the combination is excellent. Finely chopped leftover cooked meat can also be added in this way.

# Refried Bean Nachos

In this Mexican classic, refried beans and tortilla crisps are topped with luscious melted cheese, salsa and assorted toppings.

| NUTRITIONAL INFORMATION | | |
|---|---|---|
| Calories .......287 | Sugars .........2g | |
| Protein ........15g | Fat ..........15g | |
| Carbohydrate ...22g | Saturates .......7g | |

 15 mins      15 mins

### SERVES 6–8

## I N G R E D I E N T S

400 g/14 oz canned refried beans

400 g/14 oz canned pinto beans, drained

large pinch of ground cumin

large pinch of mild chilli powder

175 g/6 oz tortilla chips

225 g/8 oz grated cheese, such as Cheddar

salsa of your choice

1 avocado, stoned, diced, and tossed with
   lime juice

½ small onion or 3–5 spring onions, chopped

2 ripe tomatoes, diced

handful of shredded lettuce

3–4 tbsp chopped fresh coriander

soured cream, to serve

1 Place the refried beans in a pan with the pinto beans, cumin and chilli powder. Add enough water to make a thick, soup-like consistency, stirring gently so that the beans do not lose their texture.

2 Heat the bean mixture over a medium heat until hot, then lower the heat and keep the mixture warm while you prepare the rest of the dish.

3 Arrange half of the tortilla chips in the bottom of a flameproof casserole or gratin dish and cover with the bean

mixture. Sprinkle with the cheese and bake in a preheated oven, 200°C/400°F/ Gas Mark 6, until the cheese melts.

4 Alternatively, place the casserole under a preheated grill and cook for 5–7 minutes or until the cheese melts and lightly sizzles in places.

5 Arrange the salsa, avocado, onion, tomatoes, lettuce and fresh coriander on top of the melted cheese. Surround with the remaining tortilla chips and serve immediately with soured cream.

## VARIATION

Replace the soured cream with natural Greek-style yogurt as an alternative.

# Roasted Cheese with Salsa

This delicious, warming Mexican dish is very satisfying – the salsa is cooked with the cheese for a wonderful mingling of textures.

## NUTRITIONAL INFORMATION

| | |
|---|---|
| Calories . . . . . . .476 | Sugars . . . . . . . . .4g |
| Protein . . . . . . . .23g | Fat . . . . . . . . . .13g |
| Carbohydrate . . .70g | Saturates . . . . . . .7g |

15 mins     5–10 mins

### SERVES 4

## I N G R E D I E N T S

8 soft corn tortillas

225 g/8 oz mozzarella, fresh pecorino, or Mexican queso oaxaca

175 ml/6 fl oz Salsa Cruda (see page 16), or other good salsa

½–1 onion, finely chopped

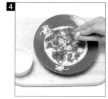

1. To warm the corn tortillas ready for serving, heat a non-stick frying pan, add a tortilla and heat through, sprinkling with a few drops of water as it heats. Wrap the tortilla in kitchen foil to keep it warm, then repeat the process with the remaining tortillas and keep them warm.

2. Cut chunks or slabs of the cheese and arrange in a shallow ovenproof dish or in individual dishes.

3. Spoon the salsa over the cheese to cover and place in either a preheated oven at 200°C/400°F/Gas Mark 6 or under a preheated grill. Cook until the cheese melts and bubbles, lightly browning in spots.

4. Sprinkle with chopped onion to taste and serve with the warmed tortillas for dipping. Serve immediately because the melted cheese turns stringy when cold and becomes difficult to eat.

### COOK'S TIP

Queso oaxaca is the authentic cheese to use, but mozzarella or pecorino make excellent substitutes since they produce the right effect when melted.

# French Bean Salad with Feta

This fresh-tasting salad is flavoured with fresh coriander, a herb that resembles flat-leaved parsley in appearance, but tastes quite different.

## NUTRITIONAL INFORMATION

Calories .......275  Sugars .........7g
Protein .........6g  Fat ..........25g
Carbohydrate ....8g  Saturates .......6g

 10 mins     5 mins

### SERVES 4

## INGREDIENTS

350 g/12 oz French beans, trimmed

1 red onion, chopped

3–4 tbsp chopped fresh coriander

2 radishes, thinly sliced

75 g/2¾ oz feta cheese, crumbled

1 tsp chopped fresh oregano or
½ tsp dried oregano

2 tbsp red wine or fruit vinegar

5 tbsp extra-virgin olive oil

3 ripe tomatoes, cut into wedges

pepper

## VARIATION

This recipe is also delicious made with nopales (edible cacti), which are available in cans or jars from specialist shops. Drain, then slice, and use instead of the French beans, missing out step 1. Replace the feta with 1–2 chopped hard-boiled eggs.

1 Bring about 5 cm/2 inches of water to the boil in the bottom of a steamer or in a medium saucepan. Add the French beans to the top of the steamer or place them in a metal colander set over the pan of water. Cover and steam for about 5 minutes until just tender.

2 Transfer the beans to a bowl and add the onion, coriander, radishes and crumbled feta cheese.

3 Sprinkle the oregano over the salad, then grind pepper over to taste. Whisk the vinegar and olive oil together and then pour over the salad. Toss gently to mix well.

4 Transfer to a serving platter, surround with the tomato wedges, and serve at once, or chill until ready to serve.

# Authentic Guacamole

Guacamole is at its best when freshly made, with enough texture so that you can really taste the avocado. Serve with vegetable sticks or tortilla chips.

## NUTRITIONAL INFORMATION

| | | |
|---|---|---|
| Calories . . . . . . . .212 | Sugars . . . . . . . . .1g | |
| Protein . . . . . . . . .2g | Fat . . . . . . . . . .21g | |
| Carbohydrate . . . .3g | Saturates . . . . . . .4g | |

 15 mins  0 mins

### SERVES 4

### I N G R E D I E N T S

1 ripe tomato

2 limes

2–3 ripe small to medium avocados, or 1–2 large ones

¼–½ onion, finely chopped

pinch of ground cumin

pinch of mild chilli powder

½–1 fresh green chilli, such as jalapeño or serrano, deseeded and finely chopped

1 tbsp finely chopped fresh coriander leaves, plus extra to garnish

salt (optional)

tortilla chips, to serve (optional)

1 Place the tomato in a heatproof bowl, pour boiling water over to cover, and leave to stand for 30 seconds. Drain and plunge into cold water. Peel off the skins. Cut the tomato in half, deseed, and chop the flesh.

2 Squeeze the juice from the limes into a small bowl. Cut 1 avocado in half around the stone. Twist the 2 halves apart in opposite directions, then remove the stone with a knife. Carefully peel off the skin, dice the flesh, and toss in the bowl of lime juice to prevent the flesh discolouring. Repeat with the remaining avocados. Mash the avocado flesh fairly coarsely with a fork.

3 Add the onion, tomato, cumin, chilli powder, fresh chilli and chopped fresh coriander to the avocados. If using as a dip for tortilla chips, do not add salt. If using as a dip for vegetable sticks, add salt to taste.

4 To serve the guacamole, transfer to a serving dish, garnish with finely chopped fresh coriander and serve with tortilla chips.

### COOK'S TIP

Try spooning guacamole into soups, especially chicken or seafood, or spreading it into sandwiches or thick crusty rolls. Spoon guacamole over refried beans and melted cheese, then eat it with salsa and crisp tortilla chips.

# Quick Tomato Sauce

This tomato sauce is very quick and very versatile – it can be served over pasta or can form the basis for spicy bean casseroles.

### NUTRITIONAL INFORMATION

Calories ........58  Sugars .........3g
Protein .........1g  Fat ...........6g
Carbohydrate ....5g  Saturates ....0.5g

 5 mins     15 mins

### SERVES 4–6

### I N G R E D I E N T S

2 tbsp vegetable oil or olive oil

1 onion, thinly sliced

5 garlic cloves, thinly sliced

400 g/14 oz canned tomatoes, diced, plus their juices, or 600 g/1 lb 5 oz diced fresh tomatoes

several shakes of mild chilli powder

350 ml/12 fl oz vegetable stock

pinch of sugar (optional)

salt and pepper

**VARIATION**
For a hotter kick, add ½ teaspoon of finely chopped fresh chilli with the onion.

1 Heat the oil in a large frying pan. Add the onion and garlic and cook, stirring, until just softened.

2 Add the tomatoes, chilli powder to taste, and the stock. Cook over a medium-high heat for 10 minutes or until the tomatoes have reduced slightly and the flavour is more concentrated.

3 Season with sugar, if using, and salt and pepper and serve warm.

# Mild Red Chilli Sauce

In this delicious recipe, the chillies are first roasted, either over a naked flame or under a grill, to give them a wonderful smoky flavour.

10 mins, plus cooling       15 mins

### MAKES 350 ML/12 FL OZ

## I N G R E D I E N T S

5 large, fresh, mild chillies, such as New Mexico or ancho

450 ml/16 fl oz vegetable stock

1 tbsp masa harina or 1 crumbled corn tortilla, puréed with enough water to make a thin paste

large pinch of ground cumin

1–2 garlic cloves, finely chopped

juice of 1 lime

salt, to taste

celery leaves, to garnish

1 Using metal tongs, roast each chilli over an open flame until darkened on all sides, or place under a preheated grill, turning frequently. Do not let them burn.

2 Put the chillies in a heatproof bowl and pour boiling water over them. Cover and leave to cool.

3 Meanwhile, put the vegetable stock in a saucepan and bring to a simmer.

4 When the chillies have cooled and are swelled up and softened, remove from the water with a slotted spoon. Remove the seeds from the chillies, then cut or tear the flesh into pieces and place in a blender or food processor. Process to form a purée, then mix in the hot stock.

5 Transfer to a saucepan. Add the masa harina or puréed tortilla, cumin, garlic and lime juice. Bring to the boil and cook for a few minutes, stirring, until the sauce has thickened. Adjust the seasoning, garnish with celery leaves and serve.

# Two Classic Salsas

A Mexican meal is not complete without an accompanying salsa.
These two salsas are ideal for seasoning any traditional dish.

## NUTRITIONAL INFORMATION

Calories . . . . . . . . .21   Sugars . . . . . . . . .3g
Protein . . . . . . . . .1g   Fat . . . . . . . . . .0g
Carbohydrate . . . .4g   Saturates . . . . . . .0g

5 mins          0 mins

### SERVES 4–6

## I N G R E D I E N T S

### JALAPEÑO SALSA

1 onion, finely chopped

2–3 garlic cloves, finely chopped

4–6 tbsp coarsely chopped pickled
   jalapeño chillies

juice of ½ lemon

about ¼ tsp ground cumin

salt

### SALSA CRUDA

6–8 ripe tomatoes, finely chopped

about 100 ml/3½ fl oz tomato juice

3–4 garlic cloves, finely chopped

½–1 bunch fresh coriander leaves,
   coarsely chopped

pinch of sugar

3–4 fresh green chillies, such as jalapeño
   or serrano, deseeded and finely chopped

½–1 tsp ground cumin

3–4 spring onions, finely chopped

salt

1 To make the jalapeño salsa, put the
onion in a non-metallic bowl with the
garlic, jalapeños, lemon juice and cumin.
Season to taste with salt and stir together.
Cover with clingfilm and chill in the
refrigerator until required.

2 To make a chunky-textured salsa
cruda, stir all the ingredients together
in a bowl and season with salt to taste.
Cover with clingfilm and chill in the
refrigerator until required.

3 To make a smoother-textured salsa,
process the ingredients in a blender
or food processor. Scrape into a bowl,
cover and chill as above.

**COOK'S TIP**
You can vary the amount of
garlic, chillies and ground spices
according to taste, but make
sure the salsa has quite a 'kick'
otherwise it will not be effective

# Vegetable Tostadas

Just top a crisp tostada (a fried tortilla) with spicy vegetables to create a magnificent Tex-Mex vegetarian feast.

   10 mins        20 mins

### SERVES 4

## I N G R E D I E N T S

4 corn tortillas

vegetable oil, for cooking

2–3 tbsp extra-virgin olive oil or
   vegetable oil

2 potatoes, diced

1 carrot, diced

3 garlic cloves, finely chopped

1 red pepper, deseeded and diced

1 tsp mild chilli powder

1 tsp paprika

½ tsp ground cumin

3–4 ripe tomatoes, diced

115 g/4 oz French beans, blanched and cut
   into bite-sized lengths

pinch of dried oregano

400 g/14 oz cooked black beans, drained

225 g/8 oz feta cheese, crumbled

3–4 leaves cos lettuce, shredded

3–4 spring onions, thinly sliced

1 To make the tostadas, cook the tortillas in a little vegetable oil in a non-stick frying pan until crisp.

2 Heat the olive oil in a frying pan, add the potatoes and carrot, and cook until softened. Add the garlic, red pepper, chilli powder, paprika and cumin. Cook for 2–3 minutes until the red pepper has softened.

3 Add the tomatoes, French beans, and oregano. Cook for 8–10 minutes until the vegetables are tender and form a sauce-like mixture. The mixture should not be too dry; add a little water if necessary, to keep it moist.

4 Heat the black beans in a saucepan with a tiny quantity of water and keep warm. Reheat the tostadas under the grill.

5 Layer the beans over the hot tostadas, sprinkle with the cheese and top with a few spoonfuls of the hot vegetables in sauce. Sprinkle over the lettuce and spring onions and serve immediately.

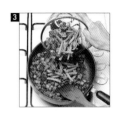

# Broccoli Enchiladas

These delicious and very nutritious enchiladas are cooked in a mild chilli sauce and served with a hot salsa.

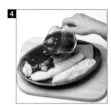

## NUTRITIONAL INFORMATION

Calories . . . . . . .605   Sugars . . . . . . . . .7g
Protein . . . . . . . .37g   Fat . . . . . . . . . .33g
Carbohydrate . . .42g   Saturates . . . . . .18g

20 mins      30 mins

### SERVES 4

## INGREDIENTS

450 g/1 lb broccoli florets

225 g/8 oz ricotta cheese

1 garlic clove, chopped

½ tsp ground cumin

175–200 g/6–7 oz Cheddar cheese, grated

6–8 tbsp freshly grated Parmesan cheese

1 egg, lightly beaten

4–6 flour tortillas

vegetable oil, for greasing

1 quantity Mild Red Chilli Sauce
(see page 15)

225 ml/8 fl oz vegetable stock

½ onion, finely chopped

3–4 tbsp chopped fresh coriander

3 tomatoes, diced

salt and pepper

hot salsa, to serve

1 Bring a saucepan of salted water to the boil, add the broccoli, bring back to the boil, and blanch for 1 minute. Drain, refresh under cold running water, then drain again. Cut off the stems, peel and chop. Dice the heads.

2 In a bowl, mix the broccoli with the ricotta cheese, garlic, cumin, and half the Cheddar cheese and Parmesan. Mix in the egg and season with salt and pepper.

3 Heat the tortillas in a lightly greased non-stick frying pan, then wrap them in foil to keep warm.

4 Fill the tortillas with the broccoli mixture, rolling them up. Arrange the tortilla rolls in an ovenproof dish, then pour the red chilli sauce over the top. Pour over the stock.

5 Top with the remaining grated cheeses and bake in a preheated oven, 190°C/375°F/Gas Mark 5, for about 30 minutes.

6 Sprinkle over the chopped onion, fresh coriander and diced tomatoes, and serve with a hot salsa.

# Mexican Refried Beans

These are refried beans fit for a fiesta, rich with everything – bacon, cooked onions, tomatoes, even some beer; as delicious as it sounds!

## NUTRITIONAL INFORMATION

| | | | |
|---|---|---|---|
| Calories | .......290 | Sugars | ........7g |
| Protein | ........16g | Fat | ..........12g |
| Carbohydrate | ...27g | Saturates | ......3g |

10 mins    20 mins

### SERVES 4

## I N G R E D I E N T S

1–2 tbsp vegetable oil

1–1½ large onions, chopped

125 g/4½ oz bacon lardons or bacon cut into small pieces

3–4 garlic cloves, finely chopped

about 1 tsp ground cumin

½ tsp mild chilli powder

400 g/14 oz canned tomatoes, diced and drained, reserving about 150–175 ml/ 5–6 fl oz of their juices

400 g/14 oz canned refried beans, broken up into pieces

100 ml/3½ fl oz beer

400 g/14 oz canned pinto beans, drained

salt and pepper

### TO SERVE

warmed flour tortillas

soured cream

pickled chillies, sliced

 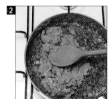 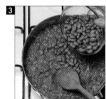

1 Heat the oil in a frying pan. Add the chopped onions and the bacon and cook for about 5 minutes until they are just turning brown. Stir in the garlic, cumin and chilli powder and continue to cook for a minute. Add the tomatoes and cook over a medium-high heat until the liquid has evaporated.

2 Add the refried beans and mash lightly in the pan with the tomato mixture, adding beer as needed to thin out the beans and make them smoother. Lower the heat and cook, stirring, until the mixture is smooth and creamy.

3 Add the pinto beans and stir well to combine; if the mixture is too thick, add a little of the reserved tomato juice. Adjust the spices to taste. Season with salt and pepper and serve with warmed tortillas, soured cream and pickled chillies.

### VARIATION

Top the dish with grated cheese, then pop under a preheated grill to melt and sizzle. Serve at once. This makes a luscious filling for warm flour tortillas.

# Rice with Black Beans

Any kind of bean cooking liquid is delicious for cooking rice – black beans are particularly good for their startling grey colour and earthy flavour.

## NUTRITIONAL INFORMATION

| | | |
|---|---|---|
| Calories .......252 | Sugars .........2g | |
| Protein .........5g | Fat ...........8g | |
| Carbohydrate ...43g | Saturates .......1g | |

🍲 15 mins     ⏱ 15 mins

---

### SERVES 4

## I N G R E D I E N T S

1 onion, chopped

5 garlic cloves, chopped

225 ml/8 fl oz chicken stock or vegetable stock

2 tbsp vegetable oil

175 g/6 oz long-grain rice

225 ml/8 fl oz liquid from cooking black beans (including some black beans, too)

½ tsp ground cumin

salt and pepper

### TO GARNISH

3–5 spring onions, thinly sliced

2 tbsp chopped fresh coriander leaves

1 Put the onion in a blender or food processor with the garlic and stock and process to a chunky sauce.

2 Heat the oil in a heavy-based frying pan. Add the rice and cook over a low heat, stirring constantly, until it is golden. Add the onion mixture, with the cooking liquid from the black beans (and some beans, too). Add the cumin and season with salt and pepper to taste.

3 Cover the pan and cook over a low heat for about 10 minutes or until the rice is just tender. The rice should be a greyish colour and taste delicious.

4 Fluff up the rice with a fork, replace the cover, and set aside to rest for about 5 minutes. Transfer to a serving dish and serve garnished with thinly sliced spring onions and the chopped fresh coriander leaves.

## VARIATION

Instead of black beans, you can use pinto beans or chickpeas instead. Proceed as above and serve with any savoury spicy sauce or as an accompaniment to roasted meat.

# Crab & Avocado Soft Tacos

Crab and avocado make an elegant yet authentic filling for tacos. Taste and you will be transported to a beach somewhere south of Acapulco!

| NUTRITIONAL INFORMATION | |
| --- | --- |
| Calories . . . . . . .522 | Sugars . . . . . . . . .4g |
| Protein . . . . . . . .22g | Fat . . . . . . . . . .19g |
| Carbohydrate . . .69g | Saturates . . . . . . .7g |

🍳 10–15 mins   🕐 10 mins

## SERVES 4

## I N G R E D I E N T S

8 corn tortillas

1 avocado

lime or lemon juice, for tossing

4–6 tbsp soured cream

250–275 g/9–10 oz cooked crab meat

½ lime

½ fresh green chilli, such as jalapeño or serrano, deseeded, and chopped or thinly sliced

1 ripe tomato, deseeded and diced

½ small onion, finely chopped

2 tbsp chopped fresh coriander

salsa of your choice (optional)

sliced radishes, to garnish (optional)

1 Heat the tortillas in an ungreased non-stick frying pan, sprinkling them with a few drops of water as they heat; wrap them in a clean tea towel as you work to keep them warm.

2 Cut the avocado in half around the stone. Twist apart, then remove the stone with a knife. Carefully peel off the skin from the avocado, slice the flesh, and toss in lime or lemon juice to prevent it from turning brown.

3 Spread 1 tortilla with soured cream. Top with crab meat, a squeeze of lime juice and a sprinkling of chilli, tomato, onion, coriander and avocado. Add a splash of salsa, if using. Repeat the procedure with the remaining tortillas. Garnish with sliced radishes, if using, and serve immediately.

### VARIATION

For tostadas, cook the tortillas in a little oil in a non-stick pan until crisp. Top one crisp tortilla with the filling. Prepare a second tortilla with the filling and place on top of the first. Repeat once more, to make a small tower, top with shredded lettuce, and serve.

# Fish Burritos

You can use any fish you like in this tasty Mexican snack, which is the Tex-Mex equivalent of a delicious sandwich

| NUTRITIONAL INFORMATION | |
|---|---|
| Calories .......269 | Sugars .........3g |
| Protein ........20g | Fat ...........2g |
| Carbohydrate ...46g | Saturates .......0g |

45 mins

10–15 mins

### SERVES 4–6

## INGREDIENTS

about 450 g/1 lb firm-fleshed white fish, such as red snapper or cod

¼ tsp ground cumin

pinch of dried oregano

4 garlic cloves, finely chopped

125 ml/4 fl oz fresh fish stock, or water mixed with a fish stock cube

juice of ½ lemon or lime

8 flour tortillas

2–3 leaves cos lettuce, shredded

2 ripe tomatoes, diced

Salsa Cruda (see page 16)

salt and pepper

### TO SERVE

slices of fresh lemon

mixed salad leaves

## VARIATION

Cook several peeled waxy potatoes in the fish stock, then dice and serve wrapped up in the warm tortillas with the lettuce, fish, tomato and salsa. Alternatively, add sliced lime-dressed avocado with the filling.

1 Season the fish to taste with salt and pepper, then put in a saucepan with the cumin, oregano, garlic and enough fish stock to cover.

2 Bring to the boil and cook for about a minute. Remove the pan from the heat and set the fish aside to cool in the cooking liquid for about 30 minutes.

3 Remove the fish from the stock and break up into bite-sized pieces. Sprinkle with the lemon or lime juice and set aside.

4 Heat the tortillas in an ungreased non-stick frying pan, sprinkling them with a few drops of water as they heat. Wrap them in a clean tea towel as you work to keep them warm.

5 Arrange shredded lettuce in the middle of a tortilla, spoon on a few chunks of the fish, then sprinkle with tomato. Add a little Salsa Cruda. Repeat with the other tortillas and serve immediately with lemon slices and mixed salad leaves.

# Chicken Tacos from Puebla

Seasoned chicken fills these soft tacos, along with creamy refried beans, avocado, smoky chipotle and soured cream.

## NUTRITIONAL INFORMATION

| Calories | .......674 | Sugars | .........6g |
|---|---|---|---|
| Protein | ........34g | Fat | ..........25g |
| Carbohydrate | ...80g | Saturates | .......9g |

🍲 10 mins    🕐 15 mins

### SERVES 4

## INGREDIENTS

8 corn tortillas

2 tsp vegetable oil

225–350 g/8–12 oz cooked chicken, diced or shredded

225 g/8 oz canned refried beans, warmed with 2 tbsp water

¼ tsp ground cumin

¼ tsp dried oregano

1 avocado, stoned, peeled, sliced, and tossed with lime juice

1 quantity Jalapeño Salsa (see page 16), or other salsa of your choice

1 canned chipotle chilli in adobo marinade or bottled chipotle salsa, chopped

175 ml/6 fl oz soured cream

½ onion, chopped

handful of lettuce leaves, shredded

5 radishes, diced

salt and pepper

1 Heat the tortillas in a stack in an ungreased non-stick frying pan, alternating the top and bottom tortillas so that they all heat evenly. Wrap in kitchen foil or a clean tea towel to keep warm.

2 Heat the oil in a frying pan, add the chicken and heat through. Season with salt and pepper to taste.

3 Combine the refried beans with the cumin and oregano.

4 Spread a tortilla with warm refried beans, then top with a spoonful of the chicken, 1–2 slices of avocado, a dab of Jalapeño Salsa, chipotle to taste, a spoonful of soured cream, and a sprinkling of onion, lettuce and radishes. Season to taste, then roll up tightly. Repeat with the remaining tortillas and serve immediately.

### VARIATION
Replace the chicken with 450 g/1 lb minced beef browned with a seasoning of chopped onion, mild chilli powder, and ground cumin to taste.

# Chicken Tostadas

Chicken makes a delicate, yet satisfying topping for crisp tostadas. Leftover cooked chicken can also be used and tastes delicious.

## NUTRITIONAL INFORMATION

| | | | |
|---|---|---|---|
| Calories | .......663 | Sugars | .........3g |
| Protein | ........45g | Fat | .........32g |
| Carbohydrate | ...49g | Saturates | ......11g |

 20 mins    🕐 10–15 mins

### SERVES 4–6

### I N G R E D I E N T S

vegetable oil, for cooking

6 corn tortillas

450 g/1 lb skinless, boneless chicken breast or thigh, cut into strips or diced

225 ml/8 fl oz chicken stock

2 garlic cloves, finely chopped

400 g/14 oz canned refried beans

2 tbsp water

large pinch of ground cumin

225 g/8 oz cheese, grated

1 tbsp chopped fresh coriander

2 ripe tomatoes, diced

crisp lettuce leaves, such as cos or iceberg, shredded

4–6 radishes, diced

3 spring onions, thinly sliced

1 ripe avocado, stoned, peeled, and diced or sliced, then tossed with lime juice

soured cream, to taste

1–2 canned chipotle chillies in adobo marinade, cut into thin strips

1 To make tostadas, heat a small amount of oil in a heavy non-stick frying pan and cook the tortillas, in batches, until crisp.

2 Put the chicken in a saucepan with the stock and garlic. Bring to the boil, then lower the heat and simmer for 1–2 minutes, until the chicken begins to turn opaque.

3 Remove the chicken from the heat and set aside to steep in the hot liquid and cook through.

4 Gently heat the beans with the water. Stir in the cumin and keep warm.

5 Reheat the tostadas under a preheated grill, if necessary. Spread the hot beans on the tostadas, then sprinkle with the grated cheese. Lift the cooked chicken from the cooking liquid with a slotted spoon and divide among the tostadas. Top with the chopped fresh coriander, diced tomatoes, shredded lettuce, diced radishes, sliced spring onions, avocado, soured cream and a few strips of chipotle chilli. Serve immediately.

# Tequila Chicken Wings

Tequila tenderizes these tasty chicken wings. Serve accompanied by corn tortillas, refried beans, salsa and lots of chilled beer.

## NUTRITIONAL INFORMATION

Calories . . . . . . .489  Sugars . . . . . . . . .8g
Protein . . . . . . . .41g  Fat . . . . . . . . . .30g
Carbohydrate . . . .11g  Saturates . . . . . . .7g

5 mins, plus 3 hrs marinating  |  15–20 mins

### SERVES 4

## I N G R E D I E N T S

900 g/2 lb chicken wings

### M A R I N A D E

11 garlic cloves, finely chopped

juice of 2 limes

juice of 1 orange

2 tbsp tequila

1 tbsp mild chilli powder

2 dried chipotle chillies, reconstituted and puréed

2 tbsp vegetable oil

1 tsp sugar

¼ tsp ground mixed spice

pinch of ground cinnamon

pinch of ground cumin

pinch of dried oregano

1 Cut the chicken wings into two pieces at the joint.

2 To make the marinade, put all the ingredients in a non-metallic dish and mix until thoroughly combined. Add the chicken wings, toss well to coat, then place in the refrigerator to marinate for at least 3 hours, or preferably overnight.

3 Cook the chicken wings over hot coals or in a ridged grill pan, turning occasionally, for about 15–20 minutes or until the wings are crisply browned. To test whether the chicken is cooked, pierce a thick part with a skewer – the juices should run clear. Serve immediately.

## COOK'S TIP

Tequila, Mexico's famous alcoholic drink, is made from the agave plant.

# Lamb & Black Bean Burritos

Stir-fried marinated lamb strips are paired with earthy black beans in these tasty filled tortillas.

## NUTRITIONAL INFORMATION

| | | | |
|---|---|---|---|
| Calories | . . . . . . . .551 | Sugars | . . . . . . . . .4g |
| Protein | . . . . . . . .45g | Fat | . . . . . . . . . .19g |
| Carbohydrate | . . .52g | Saturates | . . . . . . .7g |

4¼ hrs    15–20 mins

### SERVES 4

## INGREDIENTS

650 g/1 lb 7 oz lean lamb

400 g/14 oz cooked or canned black beans, seasoned with cumin, salt and pepper

2 tbsp water

4 large flour tortillas

2–3 tbsp chopped fresh coriander, plus extra to garnish

4–6 tbsp salsa of your choice

salt and pepper

wedges of lime, to serve

### MARINADE

3 garlic cloves, finely chopped

juice of ½ lime

½ tsp mild chilli powder

½ tsp ground cumin

pinch of dried oregano

1–2 tbsp extra-virgin olive oil

## VARIATION

Add a spoonful or two of cooked rice to each burrito.

1 Slice the lamb into thin strips. To make the marinade, put the garlic, lime juice, chilli powder, cumin, oregano and olive oil in a non-metallic bowl. Add the lamb and season with salt and pepper. Marinate in the refrigerator for 4 hours.

2 Put the black beans and water in a pan and warm gently.

3 Heat the tortillas in an ungreased non-stick frying pan, sprinkling with a few drops of water as they heat; wrap them in a clean tea towel as you work to keep them

warm. Alternatively, heat through in a stack in the frying pan, alternating the top and bottom tortillas so that they warm evenly.

4 Stir-fry the lamb in a heavy non-stick frying pan over a high heat until browned on all sides. Remove from the heat.

5 Spoon some of the beans and browned meat into a tortilla, sprinkle with coriander, then top with salsa and roll up. Repeat with the remaining tortillas, garnish with coriander and serve immediately with wedges of lime.

# Classic Beef Fajitas

Sizzling marinated strips of meat rolled up in soft flour tortillas with a tangy salsa are a real Mexican treat, perfect for relaxed entertaining.

| NUTRITIONAL INFORMATION | | | |
|---|---|---|---|
| Calories | .......623 | Sugars | .........6g |
| Protein | ........36g | Fat | ..........23g |
| Carbohydrate | ...72g | Saturates | .......7g |

 45 mins    15–20 mins

### SERVES 4–6

## I N G R E D I E N T S

700 g/1 lb 9 oz steak

12 flour tortillas

vegetable oil, for cooking

1–2 avocados, stoned, peeled, and sliced, then tossed with lime juice

125 ml/4 fl oz soured cream

salt and pepper

### M A R I N A D E

6 garlic cloves, chopped

juice of 1 lime

pinch of mild chilli powder

pinch of paprika

pinch of ground cumin

1–2 tbsp extra-virgin olive oil

### P I C O  D E  G A L L O  S A L S A

8 ripe tomatoes, diced

3 spring onions, sliced

1–2 fresh green chillies, such as jalapeño or serrano, deseeded and chopped

3–4 tbsp chopped fresh coriander

5–8 radishes, diced

ground cumin, to taste

1 Cut the beef into strips. To make the marinade, put all the ingredients in a non-metallic bowl. Add the beef and salt and pepper, mix well, and marinate for at least 30 minutes at room temperature or up to 8 hours in the refrigerator.

2 To make the salsa, put all the ingredients in a bowl. Season to taste.

3 Heat the tortillas in a lightly greased non-stick frying pan. Wrap in kitchen foil as you work, to keep them warm.

4 Stir-fry the meat in a little oil over a high heat until browned and just cooked through.

5 Transfer the sizzling hot meat, warm tortillas, salsa, avocado and soured cream to separate serving dishes, for each person to serve themselves and make their own rolled up fajitas.

# Chilli con Carne

This is probably the best-known Mexican dish and one that is a great favourite with all. The chilli content can be increased to suit your taste.

## NUTRITIONAL INFORMATION

| | | | |
|---|---|---|---|
| Calories | .......443 | Sugars | ........11g |
| Protein | ........48g | Fat | ..........15g |
| Carbohydrate | ...30g | Saturates | ......4g |

5 mins    2½ hrs

### SERVES 4

## I N G R E D I E N T S

750 g/1 lb 10 oz lean braising or stewing steak

2 tbsp vegetable oil

1 large onion, sliced

2–4 garlic cloves, crushed

1 tbsp plain flour

425 ml/15 fl oz tomato juice

400 g/14 oz canned tomatoes

1–2 tbsp sweet chilli sauce

1 tsp ground cumin

425 g/15 oz canned red kidney beans, drained

½ tsp dried oregano

1–2 tbsp chopped fresh parsley

salt and pepper

sprigs of fresh herbs, to garnish

boiled rice and warmed tortillas, to serve

 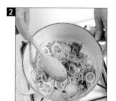 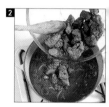

## COOK'S TIP

Since chilli con carne requires quite a lengthy cooking time, it saves time and fuel to prepare double the quantity you need and freeze half of it to serve on another occasion. Thaw and use within 3–4 weeks.

1 Cut the beef into 2-cm/¾-inch cubes. Heat the oil in a flameproof casserole and cook the beef until well sealed. Remove from the casserole.

2 Add the onion and garlic to the casserole and cook until lightly browned. Stir in the flour and cook for 1–2 minutes. Stir in the tomato juice and tomatoes and bring to the boil. Replace the beef and add the chilli sauce, cumin and seasoning. Cover and place in a preheated oven, 160°C/325°F/Gas Mark 3, for 1½ hours or until almost tender.

3 Stir in the beans, oregano and parsley and adjust the seasoning. Cover the casserole and return to the oven for 45 minutes. Garnish with herb sprigs and serve with boiled rice and warmed tortillas.

# Spicy Meat & Chipotle Hash

This speciality from the Puebla in Mexico makes divine soft tacos: simply serve with a stack of warm corn tortillas and let everyone roll their own.

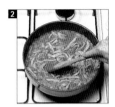

| NUTRITIONAL INFORMATION | |
|---|---|
| Calories . . . . . . . .210 | Sugars . . . . . . . . .3g |
| Protein . . . . . . . .26g | Fat . . . . . . . . . . .10g |
| Carbohydrate . . . .4g | Saturates . . . . . . .4g |

10 mins        15–20 mins

## SERVES 6

## I N G R E D I E N T S

1 tbsp vegetable oil

1 onion, finely chopped

450 g/1 lb leftover cooked meat, cooled and cut into thin strips

1 tbsp mild chilli powder

2 ripe tomatoes, deseeded and diced

about 225 ml/8 fl oz meat stock

½–1 canned chipotle chilli, mashed, plus a little adobo sauce, or a dash of chipotle salsa

chopped fresh coriander, to garnish

### TO SERVE

12 corn tortillas, warmed

125 ml/4 fl oz soured cream

4–6 tbsp chopped fresh coriander

4–6 tbsp chopped radishes

3–4 crisp lettuce leaves, shredded

1 Heat the oil in a frying pan, add the onion, and cook over a low heat, stirring occasionally, for 5 minutes until softened. Add the meat and sauté, stirring frequently, for about 3 minutes until lightly browned.

2 Add the chilli powder, tomatoes and meat stock, and cook, mashing the meat gently, until the tomatoes have disintegrated and reduced to a sauce.

3 Add the chipotle chilli or salsa and continue to cook and mash until the sauce and meat are nearly blended.

4 Serve the dish garnished with chopped coriander, accompanied by a stack of warmed corn tortillas so that people can fill them with the meaty mixture to make tacos. Also serve with soured cream, more chopped coriander, radishes and shredded lettuce for each person to add to the meat.

### COOK'S TIP

Avocados add an interesting texture contrast to the spicy meat – serve with 2 sliced avocados, tossed with lime juice. Try serving on top of tostadas (crisply fried tortillas) instead of wrapping taco-style.

# Banana Empanadas

Filo pastry makes these empanadas light and crisp on the outside, while the filling melts into a delicious hot banana-chocolate sauce.

## NUTRITIONAL INFORMATION

| | | |
|---|---|---|
| Calories | ......408 | Sugars ........40g |
| Protein | .........6g | Fat ..........17g |
| Carbohydrate | ...60g | Saturates .....10g |

🗄 10 mins    ⏱ 15 mins

### SERVES 4

## INGREDIENTS

about 8 sheets of filo pastry, cut in
  half lengthways

melted butter or vegetable oil, for brushing

2 ripe sweet bananas

1–2 tsp sugar

juice of ½ lemon

175–200 g/6–7 oz plain chocolate, chopped
  into small pieces

icing sugar and ground cinnamon,
  for dusting

**COOK'S TIP**
You could use ready-made puff
pastry instead of filo for a more
puffed-up effect.

1 Working one at a time, lay a long rectangular sheet of filo pastry out in front of you and then brush it with butter or vegetable oil.

2 Peel and dice the bananas and place in a bowl. Add the sugar and lemon juice and stir well to combine. Stir in the chocolate.

3 Place a couple of teaspoons of the banana and chocolate mixture in one corner of the filo pastry, then fold over into a triangle shape to enclose the filling. Continue to fold in a triangular shape until the pastry is completely wrapped around the filling.

4 Dust the parcels with icing sugar and cinnamon. Place them on a baking sheet and continue the process with the remaining filo pastry and filling.

5 Bake the parcels in a preheated oven, 190°C/375°F/Gas Mark 5, for about 15 minutes or until they are golden. Remove from the oven and serve immediately – warn people that the filling is very hot.

# Churros

These Mexican treats are like crisp little doughnuts,
but with a delicious lemon and spice flavour.

## NUTRITIONAL INFORMATION

| | | | |
|---|---|---|---|
| Calories | .......439 | Sugars | .......0.5g |
| Protein | ........9g | Fat | .........35g |
| Carbohydrate | ...24g | Saturates | ......15g |

 15 mins        15 mins

### SERVES 4

## I N G R E D I E N T S

225 ml/8 fl oz water

zest of 1 lemon

6 tbsp butter

⅛ tsp salt

125 g/4½ oz plain flour

¼ tsp ground cinnamon, plus extra
for dusting

½–1 tsp vanilla extract

3 eggs

oil, for cooking

about 5 tbsp sugar

1 Place the water with the lemon zest in a heavy saucepan. Bring to the boil, add the butter and salt, and cook for a few moments until the butter melts.

2 Add the flour all at once, with the cinnamon and vanilla extract, then remove the pan from the heat and stir rapidly until the mixture forms the consistency of mashed potatoes.

3 Beat in the eggs, one at a time, using a wooden spoon; if you have difficulty incorporating the eggs to a smooth mixture, use a potato masher, and then, when they are mixed, return to a wooden spoon and mix until smooth.

4 Heat 2.5 cm/1 inch of oil in a deep frying pan until it is hot enough to brown a cube of bread in 30 seconds.

5 Place the batter in a piping bag with a wide nozzle, then squeeze out 13-cm/5-inch lengths directly into the hot oil, making sure that the churros are about 7.5–10 cm/3-4 inches apart, because they will puff up as they cook. You may need cook them in 2 or 3 batches.

6 Cook the churros in the hot oil for about 2 minutes on each side until golden brown. Remove from the pan with a slotted spoon and drain on kitchen paper.

7 Dust generously with sugar and sprinkle with cinnamon to taste. Serve either hot or at room temperature.

# Margaritas

A Margarita is what makes a hot and sultry Mexican afternoon not only tolerable, but something to enjoy. A tropical holiday in a glass.

## NUTRITIONAL INFORMATION

| | | | |
|---|---|---|---|
| Calories | .......120 | Sugars | .........7g |
| Protein | .........0g | Fat | ...........0g |
| Carbohydrate | ....7g | Saturates | ......0g |

5 mins     0 mins

### SERVES 2

## I N G R E D I E N T S

### C L A S S I C   M A R G A R I T A S

pared lime or lemon rind, for moistening

salt, for dipping

3 tbsp tequila

3 tbsp orange-flavoured liqueur

3 tbsp freshly squeezed lime juice

handful of cracked ice

fine strips of lime zest, to decorate

### M E L O N   M A R G A R I T A S

1 small, flavourful cantaloupe melon, peeled, deseeded and diced

several large handfuls of ice

juice of 1 lime

100 ml/3½ fl oz tequila

sugar, to taste

### F R O Z E N   P E A C H   M A R G A R I T A S

1 peach, sliced and frozen, or an equal amount of purchased frozen peaches

50 ml/2 fl oz tequila

50 ml/2 fl oz peach liqueur or orange-flavoured liqueur

juice of ½ lime

diced fresh peach or 1–2 tbsp orange juice, if needed

1 To make the classic margaritas, moisten the rims of two shallow, stemmed glasses with the lime or lemon rind, then dip the rims of the glasses in salt. Shake off the excess.

2 Put the tequila in a blender or food processor with the liqueur, lime juice and cracked ice. Process to blend well.

3 Pour the drink into the prepared glasses, taking care not to disturb the salt-coated rim. If preferred, strain the drink before pouring into the glass. Decorate with strips of lime zest and serve.

4 To make the melon margaritas, put the melon in a food processor and process to form a purée. Add the ice, lime juice, tequila, and sugar to taste, and process until smooth. Pour into chilled shallow glasses.

5 To make the frozen peach margaritas, blend the frozen peaches with the tequila, liqueur and lime juice in a food processor until you have a thick purée. If too thick, add diced peach or orange juice to thin. Pour into chilled glasses and serve.

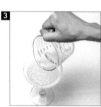